TIMELINES IN SCIENCE

SCIENCE OF THE MIDDLE AGES

Craig Boutland

ROSEN PUBLISHING

Published in 2025 by The Rosen Publishing Group, Inc.
2544 Clinton Street, Buffalo, NY 14224

Portions of this work were originally authored by Charlie Samuels and published as *Medieval Science*. All new material in this edition was authored by Craig Boutland.

PICTURE CREDITS
t=top, b=bottom, l=left, r=right, c=center

Front Cover: Shutterstock: Chantall tr, Michael Klosch-Tragaser tc, maradon33 main, Alexandre.ROSA cl.
Inside: Alamy: History and Art Collection 26, 50, World Archive/Zurich Zentralbibiotheck 51; iStockphoto: Bufi 61b, Kastelein 34t; Public Domain: Cremonensis/World ImagingGerardus 6, Derby Museum and Art Gallery 53, Museum Sztuki w Lodzi/ms/Herbst Palace/czytanieobrazow.pl 52, Thinkstock/Creatas 17, 47, Thinkstock/Photos.com 8, 10, 32bl, 61t; Shutterstock: beast01 43t, Cosma 11, Kedar Dome 29, Elen418 58, Elena Elisseeva 35, fotohunter 38, Jaroslaw Grudzinski 59, Jeff Gynane 39t, 60, haveseen 46, Steve Hiscock 18, Steffen Hoejager 15, Inga Ivanova 9t, Rich Koele 21, Lagui 55, Philip Lange 30, Michael Levy 23t, Lotus Studio 49, Macka 22, Andreas Meyer 36, Alan Morris 25, Andrea Paggiaro 37, Andrew Park 13t, Mauro Rodrigues 28, Prachaya Roekdeethaweesab 9br, Route66 23b, Tamara Rulikova 54, David Steele 27, Tandem 19, Titelio 20, Vesilvio 5, Nils Volkmer 14, Marco van Vurien 7.

All other artwork and illustrations Brown Bear Books Ltd

Cataloging-in-Publication Data

Names: Boutland, Craig.
Title: Science of the Middle Ages / Craig Boutland.
Description: Buffalo, NY : Rosen Young Adult, 2025. | Series: Timelines in science | Includes glossary and index.
Identifiers: ISBN 9781499477672 (pbk.) | ISBN 9781499477689 (library bound) | ISBN 9781499477696 (ebook)
Subjects: LCSH: Science, Medieval–Juvenile literature. | Technology–History–To 1500–Juvenile literature.
Classification: LCC Q124.97 B68 2025 | DDC 509'.02–dc23

Manufactured in the United States of America

CPSIA Compliance Information: Batch #CSRYA25.
For further information, contact Rosen Publishing at 1-800-237-9932.

CONTENTS

Introduction

The Middle Ages were a period of great advances in medicine, math, architecture, and technology as people tried to understand the world around them.

In the past, it was sometimes fashionable to see medieval science as little more than superstition and magic, full of alchemists searching for eternal life or trying to turn lead into gold. Today, historians understand that the Middle Ages were actually a period of important steps forward in both practical technology, such as the building of windmills to grind grain for food, and in theory, such as the development of mathematics and algebra.

Record Keeping

Classical knowledge recorded by the ancient Greeks and Romans virtually disappeared from Europe after the fall of the Roman Empire in 476. In the Islamic world, however, scholars preserved, translated, and spread this ancient learning. In China, meanwhile, paper was invented early in the period, eventually making it easier for discoveries to be recorded and passed on. Much technological development was gradual, with a series of tiny changes and adaptations leading over a long period of time to significant improvements to traditional tools or buildings. However, the spread of record keeping has also preserved the names of some individuals who made significant breakthroughs and discoveries.

About This Book

This book uses timelines to describe the developments in scientific knowledge and technology from about 500 to about 1500. A continuous timeline of the whole period runs along the bottom of all the pages. Its entries are color-coded to indicate the different fields of science to which the developments belong. Each chapter also has a subject-specific timeline, which runs vertically down the edge of the page.

Machines helped measure natural phenomena. This 1344 Italian clock showed not only the time, but also the phases of the moon and the positions of the sun in the zodiac.

Islamic Science

From about 750 CE, science flourished under the Abbasid caliphs of Baghdad. Drawing on ancient Greek and Hindu texts, Muslim scholars also added their own discoveries.

In this medieval illustration, the Persian physician Rhazes examines a patient.

TIMELINE
500-534

KEY:

Life Sciences

Engineering and Technology

Astronomy and Math

500 Cultivation of silkworms begins in Byzantium (now Istanbul), when Christian monks smuggle silkworms out of China.

500 In China, paddle boats using wheels along the sides of the hull are in use.

500

500 In modern-day Ecuador, the Manteño people make thin copper ax heads, which they probably use as money.

Mosques like this one in Damascus, Syria, were medieval centers of education.

Following the prophet Muhammad's return to Mecca in 630 CE, followers spread his teachings throughout a vast empire from central Asia to Spain. The Muslim conquerors did not destroy cultures, but absorbed much from them. The rise of Islam saw an increase in learning.

Science and the Umayyads

Damascus was the first Muslim capital under the Umayyad Dynasty, but in 750, the Umayyads were overthrown and the capital moved to Baghdad under the Abassid caliphs. The seventh caliph, Abdallah al-Ma'mun, was one of the greatest. Around 820, he commissioned an astronomical observatory and library as part of the Bayt al-Hikma academy (The House of Wisdom). His astronomers calculated the angle between Earth's rotational axis and its orbital plane and his geometers calculated the circumference and radius of Earth. Their calculations were almost accurate.

Timeline

622 Muhammad's flight from Mecca to Medina

630 Muhammad's return to Mecca

750 Umayyad Dynasty overthrown; capital moves from Damascus to Baghdad under Abassid caliphs

c.820 Bayt al-Hikma (The House of Wisdom) established in Baghdad

c.830 Hindu numerals introduced

c.860 Medicine according to principles of Hippocrates practiced in Baghdad

c.880 Al-Battani (Albategnius) calculates the length of the year and the times of the equinoxes

c.900 Plaster of Paris used to support fractured bones

510 520 532 534

510 Craftsmen at Gaza, in what is now Palestine, construct a complicated water clock that chimes to mark the passing of time.

520 The Roman philosopher Boethius translates many of the works of Aristotle from Greek into Latin, providing the main source of the works to later scholars.

532 Isidorus of Miletus designs the domed church of Hagia Sophia in Byzantium (present-day Istanbul). It is now a mosque.

534 Japanese mathematicians begin using Chinese math.

Ptolemy, the Greatest

Astronomers in Arabia preserved the ideas of the Greek astronomer Ptolemy, which he set out in a book in 150 CE. Ptolemy's admirers often called the book *Megiste* (greatest), and when it was translated into Arabic in about 827, it was given the Arabic al ("the") to make the title *Almagest*, by which it has been known ever since.

Ptolemy still influenced geography and astronomy many centuries after his death.

Arabian alchemist Abu Musa Jabir ibn-Hayyan, known as Geber, expanded the Greek idea that matter is made from earth, air, fire, and water. He believed the Greek elements combined to form sulfur and mercury, which could help make any metal, including gold. He experimented with varnishes, dyes, and the refining of metals from their ores.

Medicine and Math

Abu-Bakr Muhammad ibn-Zakariya al-Razi, or Rhazes, chief physician at the hospital in Baghdad, is said to have been the first person to note that measles and smallpox were different diseases. He left detailed notes so that other scientists could learn from his work. Rhazes used plaster-of-Paris casts to hold broken bones in place. He may have been the first person to classify all substances as being animal, vegetable, or mineral.

Al-Khwarizmi continued the work of the Greek mathematician Diophantus of Alexandria, reading his works in the original Greek. At this time, few scholars in western Europe spoke Greek.

TIMELINE
535-610

KEY:
- Life Sciences
- Engineering and Technology
- Astronomy and Math

535 Chinese engineers build a machine for sifting flour; it uses a crank to turn rotary motion into back-and-forth motion.

537 In the Byzantine Empire, a floating windmill is built.

542 An epidemic of bubonic plague breaks out in the eastern Mediterranean; within two years it kills a quarter of the region's population.

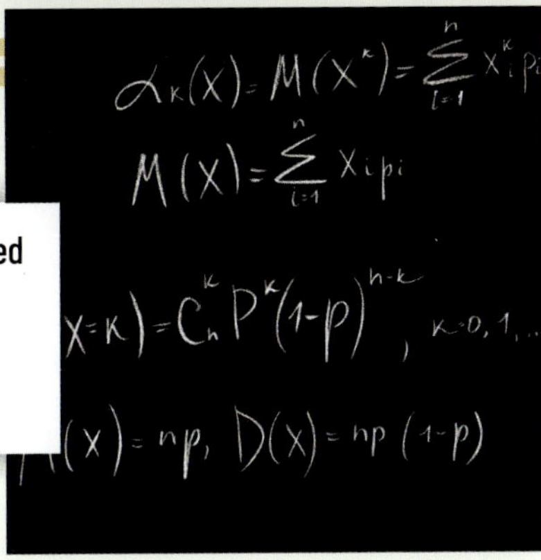

Algebra was developed by Islamic scholars to solve complex math problems.

The Coming of Algebra

Arabic scholar Abu Jafar Muhammad ibn-Musa al-Khwarizmi studied Hindu and Greek math and used Hindu numerals in his works, which were later translated into Latin. He lived in Baghdad, where he was librarian at the House of Wisdom. In about 830, he wrote a treatise on math that was highly influential. In Latin, part of its title (*al-jabr*; "restoration") became "algebra." The Latin form of al-Khwarizmi's name—Algoritmi— also gave us our word "algorithm."

Islamic Astronomy

Most astronomers accepted the Greek Ptolemy's work, but around 880, Abu-Abdullah Muhammad ibn-Jabir al-Battani, also called Albategnius, observed that when the sun appeared at its smallest—when it is farthest from Earth—its position was not where Ptolemy said it should be. Albategnius worked out that the position changes slowly. This allowed him to measure the length of the year more accurately; people making calendars were still using his measurement centuries later.

The advance of Arabian science depended on scholars translating works from Greek into Arabic. One of the greatest translators was Honain ben Isaac, a Christian physician and philosopher living in Baghdad.

This stamp showing al-Khwarizmi was issued to mark his 1,200th birthday.

550 · 577 · 605 · 610

550 In a book known as the *Book of the Golden Hall Master*, a Chinese author describes large, wind-powered carriages with sails.

577 Chinese women invent a kind of match they use to start fires for cooking.

605 In Persia (modern Iran), farmers use windmills to grind grain; unlike modern windmills, the sails are horizontal.

610 In India, mathematicians introduce a number system using base 10 (like modern math).

Making Paper

Writing is one of the greatest human inventions of all time. People needed something portable to write on. First this was papyrus; then Chinese craftsmen invented paper.

Ancient Egyptians wrote on rolls of papyrus, a kind of paper made from reeds.

TIMELINE
605-635

KEY:

Engineering and Technology

Astronomy and Math

605 The Japanese use "burning water" as fuel: it is believed to have been petroleum.

611 The Chinese build the Great Stone Bridge over the Chiao Shui River using a segmented arch; the bridge still stands.

618 Printed newspapers are produced in China.

From about 2800 BCE, the Egyptians made papyrus—which gives us the word paper—from reeds growing along the banks of the Nile River. They peeled the reeds and sliced the inner pith into strips, which were criss-crossed and pounded into a flat sheet. Then they used smooth stones to polish the dried sheets of papyrus.

Invention of Paper

Other early writing materials included tree bark, cloth, and thin animal skins made into parchment or vellum. Parchment is usually made from untanned sheepskins. It probably gets its name from the ancient Greek city of Pergamum in Asia Minor (modern Turkey) where it was made. Vellum is a similar, thinner material made from the skin of a lamb or calf. Workers clean the animal skin with lime, dry it on a frame to stretch it, and scrape it with a sharp blade to give it a smooth surface for writing on.

The first Chinese reference to paper came in about 105 CE from the writer Ts'ai Lun, who was an official at the Imperial Court during the Han Dynasty (200 BCE–220 CE). He described making paper from rags and other materials, such as tree bark, although the process probably originated at least 100 years earlier. Chinese craftsmen also made paper from leaves and other vegetable matter. One method involved taking young bamboo fibers and the inner bark of a mulberry tree and

Timeline

2800 BCE Egyptian papyrus

105 CE Chinese paper

868 First printed book

960 Paper money in China

1150 First European papermill

1442 Printing press

Early paper was more textured than modern paper, and less regular in its shape.

622 This is the first year of the Muslim calendar, marking the Prophet Muhammad's flight from Mecca to Medina.

628 Indian astronomer Brahmagupta writes a treatise on astronomy that also includes descriptions of complex math.

635 Astronomers in China observe that the tail of a comet always points away from the sun; we now know the phenomenon is due to the solar wind, a stream of charged particles emitted by the sun.

Making Paper

Papermaking has not changed much from how it was made by the Chinese in the first century CE.

(A) Material, such as leaves, mulberry bark, and bamboo shoots, was pulped using water.

(B) The papermaker spread the pulp in a thin layer onto a fine screen or mesh.

(C) The water drained away to leave a crisscross of matted fibers that dried to form a sheet of paper.

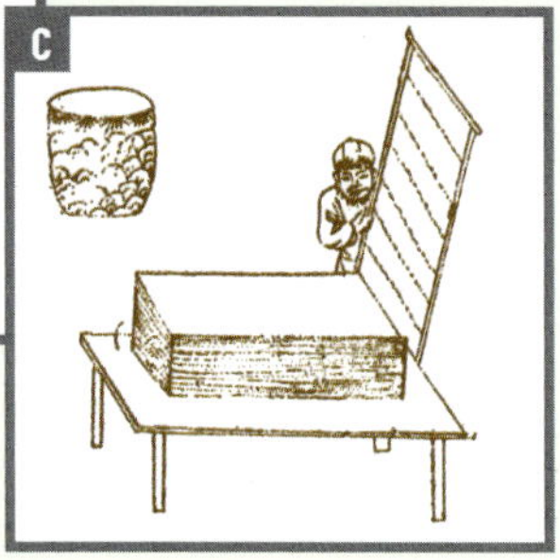

The Chinese invented papermaking in about 105 CE. Today it is made by machine, but the principle is similar.

pounding them together in water. The resulting slurry was poured through a piece of cloth stretched on a wooden frame to act as a kind of filter. The water trickled through, leaving the fibers on the cloth, which dried to form paper. They also used hemp fibers in a similar way to make a finer grade of paper, but the most expensive kind was made from silk. Coarse paper was used as wrapping paper, while soft paper was used as toilet paper.

People in other parts of the world also invented paper independently of the Chinese. Mesopotamians replaced their bulky clay tablets with a kind of reed paper resembling papyrus. By about the 6th century, inhabitants of the ancient city of Teotihuacán, Mexico, soaked and pounded fibers of fig bark to

TIMELINE
640-688

KEY:

Life Sciences

Engineering and Technology

Astronomy and Math

640

674

640 Paul of Aegina, a surgeon in the Greek city of Alexandria, writes "Seven Books of Medicine."

674 Syrian-born chemist Callinicus invents Greek fire, a flammable mixture of sulfur, resin, pitch, and saltpeter that even burns when floating in water; it helps destroy a Muslim fleet off Byzantium and becomes an important naval weapon for centuries.

In China and elsewhere, early paper could take the form of sheets or rolls.

make paper. They coated it with a chalky varnish and polished it using a smooth stone.

Knowledge of papermaking spread from China to Korea, Japan, and Vietnam from the third to the sixth centuries, then to India and Samarkand in central Asia. By the eighth century, it had reached Damascus and Baghdad in the Middle East. Arab traders spread the technique to Egypt and northern Africa by the 10th century. They used flax (linen) fibers to produce very fine, strong paper. Later, grass fibers such as esparto, straw, and eventually wood pulp were used to make paper. The first European papermaking plant was built in 1150 near Valencia, Spain. Paper factories were now mills, either because waterwheels provided the power for the pulping machines or because grindstones were used to break up the vegetable materials.

Woodblock Printing

The earliest way of printing images used woodcuts, in which a design was cut in relief on the surface of a block of wood; unwanted wood was carved away. The printer applied ink to the raised surface, then pushed the block into a sheet of paper to transfer the image.

The image on the page was a mirror image of the original image on the woodblock.

680 The Dutch build dikes to protect their low-lying land from the sea.

680 Mathematicians in Cambodia and Sumatra use the symbol 0 (zero) in calculations as a placeholder.

685 In Italy, the Ravenna Cosmography lists all the countries, rivers, and towns in the Roman empire.

688 In China, Empress Wu Tse commissions a 295-foot (90-m) pagoda constructed from cast iron.

680 685 688

Wind Power

The first windmills appeared in Persia (present-day Iran) in about 605. They were used to pump water into irrigation systems and to grind grain to make flour.

These medieval windmills stand in the breezy La Mancha region of Spain.

TIMELINE
691-725

KEY:

Engineering and Technology

691 The Dome of the Rock is completed in Jerusalem; it is made of wood and brass and covered in gold.

700 Europeans begin to use stirrups—already in use in Asia—for mounting and riding horses.

700 Spanish smiths build blast furnaces to smelt iron, using bellows to push in air to raise the temperature of the fire.

Windmills arrived in western Europe in the 12th century—soldiers fighting the Crusades probably saw them operating in the Holy Land and brought the idea home. But early European windmills differed from early Persian devices (known as panemone windmills) in one important respect: instead of being mounted on a vertical axis, European windmills had sails that radiated out from a horizontal axis, supported on the side of a post or a stone tower. This design makes much more efficient use of available air currents. On a vertical-axis panemone, only half of the sails are exposed to the wind at any time, which means that at least half the available energy is lost. By mounting the sails on a raised horizontal axis, Europeans built mills that were immediately 100 percent more efficient.

It seems puzzling that the technologically advanced Persians did not figure this out, but a horizontal-axis windmill is, in fact, a much more complex device than a vertically mounted panemone. First, using an upright

Timeline

605 Panemone mills first operated in Persia

12th century Post mills appeared in Europe for grinding grain

1414 Mills used for drainage purposes in Holland

16th century Windmill technology introduced to the New World

1772 Spring sails invented

1854 Halladay mill patented

In medieval Sweden, many farms had their own individual post mill, like this one.

720 Pyramid IV, built by the Maya of the city of Tikal (now in Guatemala), is one of the tallest buildings in Mesoamerica.

720

725

720 Buddhist charm scrolls in China feature images created by using woodblock printing.

725 Chinese engineer Liang Ling-Zan and Buddhist monk Yi-Xing build a water clock with an escapement mechanism to regulate its motion; it is not intended for timekeeping but to display various astronomical events.

Where Does the Wind Come From?

The sun heats parts of Earth's surface to different temperatures. Because warm air rises, the difference in air temperature creates pressure differences. Wind is simply air moving from an area of high pressure to an area of low pressure. The larger the pressure differential, the stronger the wind. Windmills work best in places with a strong prevailing wind. Early millers understood this and tended to build their mills on flat plains, on the coast, or on top of small hills.

In a post mill, the structure could be turned toward the breeze. Inside, gears converted the force turning the horizontal shaft into a force for turning millstones around a vertical axis.

mill to turn millstones necessitated the use of gears to move the turning force 90 degrees. For mill builders in Europe that was no problem, since the technology had already been invented for use with waterwheels. Second, an upright mill works effectively only if the sails are facing into the wind. Thus early European windmills were either built so that they faced the prevailing wind—which is the direction from which the wind normally blows—or the windmill had to be adjustable. The former solution worked well enough along the southern coasts of France and Spain and some Mediterranean islands, where the wind nearly always blew off the sea, but farther north in Europe the winds were far too variable to make this a viable solution. So

TIMELINE
750-770

KEY:

Engineering and Technology

Astronomy and Math

750 Scandinavian people are using clinker-built ships in the Baltic Sea.

750 Arab scholars moving to Spain, now partly under Muslim rule, bring knowledge of the Alexandrine school to Europe.

750

750 Craftsmen in Italy use bronze to cast large church bells.

inland mills, known as post mills, were small and mounted on a single stout post that could be turned to face the wind.

This traditional Greek windmill faces the prevailing breeze and can operate only when the wind blows from that direction.

Changing Direction

By the 15th century, windmill sails were mounted in a free-rotating cap that was separate from the main tower of the windmill. When the wind changed and the miller needed to adjust the direction the sails were facing, they only had to turn the cap, not the whole structure. This was usually done using a long pole that was attached to the back of the cap and angled down to the ground. The pole acted as a lever. Pushing the pole turned the whole cap. This advance meant that the size of windmills was no longer restricted by the need to turn them around. Mill towers could be built of brick or stone, several stories high. Now windmills were proper buildings, rather than just machines. Building them taller meant they could have larger sails and so produce more power. There was also room for the miller and their family to live and work inside the building, with different stories for different tasks, such as grinding, removing chaff from the milled flour, and bagging.

750 The traffic of goods and ideas along the Silk Road peaks at this time; the network of routes connects China with Central and South Asia, and west to the edge of Europe.

770 The Arab scholar Abu Musa Jabir ibn-Hayyan, known in the West as Geber, describes how to prepare ammonium chloride, white lead, nitric acid, and acetic acid.

750 760 770

760 The use of "Arabic" numerals—they in fact came from India—reaches as far west as Baghdad.

The Halladay Mill

The Halladay mill, patented by U.S. machinist Daniel Halladay in 1854, played a key role in the settlement of the American West. A tail fin turned the sails to follow the wind direction. Thousands of these mills still pump groundwater to the surface for livestock all over the rural United States.

The invention of the Halladay mill revolutionized livestock farming in the United States and the Australian outback.

Spring Sails

To begin with, windmills used canvas sails mounted on wooden frames. The sails would be partially furled when the wind became too strong, or they were taken off completely when the windmill was not in use. Then, in 1772, Scottish millwright Andrew Meikle invented spring sails. This marked a major change. Spring sails were made of wooden slats held shut by springs. When the wind blew hard, pressure on the sails forced the sprung slats open so that they offered less resistance. This automation ensured that the sails turned at a steady speed however the wind changed, and allowed mills to operate in gusty conditions.

TIMELINE
774-800

KEY:

Engineering and Technology

Astronomy and Math

774 Arabs begin to translate Hindu mathematical works into Arabic.

780 Arabs in Baghdad learn how to make paper from Chinese craftsmen in Samarkand, on the Silk Road.

789 Charlemagne, who rules a large empire in Europe, introduces standard weights and measures.

Further improvements followed when, in 1807, English engineer William Cubitt invented a means by which the angle of the slats, and so the speed at which the mill turned, could be adjusted while the sails were in motion. Being able to regulate the speed of the sails gave the miller much greater control over the quality of the flour he produced.

From Water to Electricity

Early windmills were used for just two purposes—pumping water and grinding grain. Nowhere were these roles more important than in Holland, where large areas of low-lying farmland were kept dry only by the constant activity of thousands of windmills that pumped out water from the fields. In the late 16th century, the invention of the crankshaft meant that windmills could also be to used to power sawmills. In Ohio in 1888, American inventor Charles Brush used a windmill to generate electricity.

Early windmills were very simple. Later mills were large enough for families to live in.

800 *Elements,* by the fourth-century BCE Greek mathematician Euclid, is translated into Arabic.

800 In Arizona, the Hohokam people build a network of canals to irrigate their crops.

800 Metalworking techniques move north from South America into Central America.

800 Native Americans in the Mississippi Valley use the bow and arrow for hunting.

800 The Arab caliph Harun al-Rashid gives Emperor Charlemagne a water clock.

Advances in Math

The European Renaissance revived learning. But the real revolution came with the invention of decimal fractions and logarithms in the 16th and 17th centuries.

The Chinese used the abacus for math calculations from about 1200 onward.

TIMELINE
812-840

KEY:

Engineering and Technology

Astronomy and Math

812 The Chinese begin to use bank drafts, the first form of money; the notes are known as "flying cash."

812 Blast furnaces are in use in Europe to make cast iron.

820 Arab mathematician Abu Jafar Muhammad ibn-Musa al- Khwarizmi describes the astrolabe.

820 A scientific academy is founded in Baghdad; it is known as the House of Wisdom.

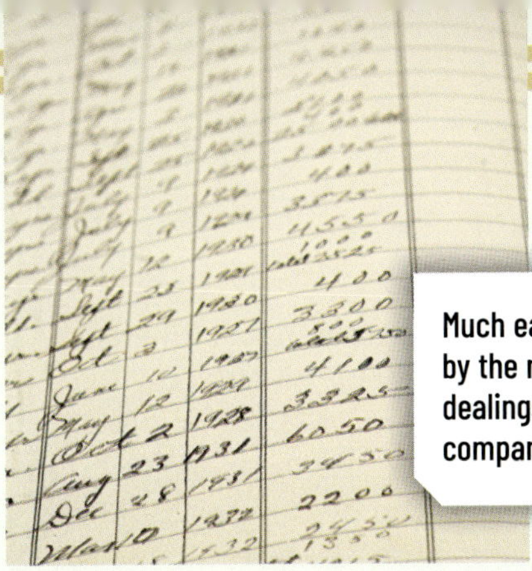

Much early math was inspired by the need to record business dealings, like this later set of company accounts.

In 1142, English philosopher Adelard of Bath translated *Elements* by Greek mathematician Euclid, making the work available to Europeans, and the astronomical tables of Abu Jafar Muhammad ibn-Musa al-Khwarizmi, copying the use of Hindu-Arabic numerals. In 1145, English scholar Robert of Chester translated al-Khwarizmi's *Hisab al-jabr w'al-muqabala (Calculation by Restoration and Reduction).*

Italian Advances

It was Leonardo Fibonacci, an Italian mathematician, who explained how to use the new numerals in *Liber Abaci (Book of Calculation)*, published in 1202. He first used a bar for fractions (¼, for example). He wrote on geometry and on number series, including the series that now bears his name, in which each number is the sum of the two preceding numbers: 0, 1, 1, 2, 3, 5, 8, 13, 21, and so on.

Timeline

1142 Latin translation of Euclid's *Elements*

1145 Latin translation of Al-Khwarizmi's *Hisab al-jabr w'al-muqabala*

1202 Fibonacci's *Liber Abaci* explains the use of Hindu-Arabic numerals

1494 Double-entry bookkeeping

1543 English book on math, *The Grounde of Artes*

1585 Decimal fractions

1591 Use of letters as quantities in algebraic equations

1594 "Natural" logarithms

1614 Tables of "natural" logarithms published

1617 Napier's "bones"

1619 Decimal point

1624 Tables of "common" logarithms

827 A second-century work by the Greek astronomer and geographer Ptolemy is translated into Arabic as *Almagest (The Greatest)*. It is highly influential in the history of astronomy.

827 834 840

834 A manuscript illustrates the use of a hand crank to turn a wheel.

840 Arab astronomers record their first sightings of sunspots.

Scholars and Merchants

All the early works were written for scholars or merchants. English scholar Robert Recorde wrote the first popular English book on mathematics, *The Grounde of Artes*. Published in 1543, it remained in print for over 150 years. Recorde was the first to use the equal (=) sign in 1557; plus (+) and minus (-) were introduced by German authors. Mathematicians wrote algebraic equations in words. In 1591, Frenchman François Viète wrote *In Artem Analytica Isogoge* (Introduction to the Analytic Art), using vowels to stand for unknown quantities and consonants for known ones, so producing the first equations that a modern mathematician would recognize. Viète is called the "father of modern algebra."

The slide rule was invented in 1622 to help in calculations; it was still used 350 years later.

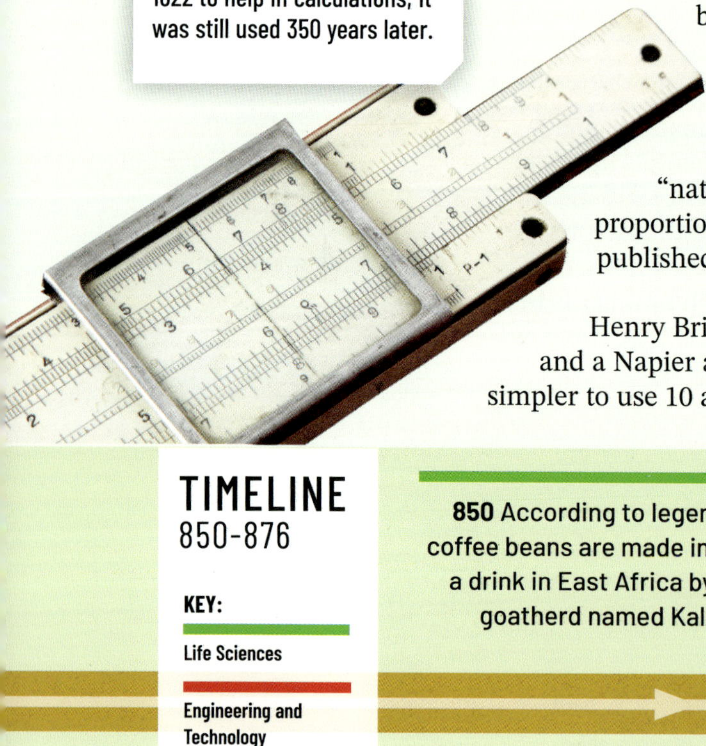

Meanwhile, in 1594 in Scotland, a brilliant mathematician named John Napier was busy devising a new method of calculation in which all numbers are expressed in exponential form. He called them "natural logarithms," meaning proportionate numbers, and in 1614, he published tables of them for everyone to use.

Henry Briggs, a professor at Oxford University and a Napier admirer, pointed out it would be simpler to use 10 as a base. Briggs had invented

TIMELINE
850-876

KEY:

Life Sciences

Engineering and Technology

Astronomy and Math

850 According to legend, coffee beans are made into a drink in East Africa by a goatherd named Kaldi.

850 Arab physician Hunayn ibn-Ishaq writes a treatise about eye problems and their treatments.

850

855

855 A Chinese pamphlet—*The Classified Essentials of the Mysterious Tao of the True Origin of Things*—describes a "fire drug," which seems to be an early form of gunpowder.

Logarithms are tables to help calculate complex math problems.

"common" logarithms. In 1624, he published a table of logarithms from 1 to 100,000. Briggs also invented the modern long division method. Simon Stevin (also known as Stevinus), introduced decimal notation into math in 1585. Decimal fractions were only used over 30 years later, however, with Napier's adoption of the decimal point.

To speed up calculations, in 1617, Napier introduced a third innovation, known as Napier's "bones," or rods. They were straight sticks with a multiplication table carved on each one. The user arranged them in a lattice pattern to solve a calculation. The answer to any long multiplication became a matter of simple addition. Around 1622, English mathematician William Oughtred invented the slide rule, which engineers and mathematicians used until the introduction of the calculator in the late 20th century.

Luca Pacioli and Accountancy

In 1494, Italian monk Luca Pacioli, considered the founder of accountancy, invented double-entry bookkeeping and described it in his book *Everything about Arithmetic, Geometry, and Proportion.* Pacioli classed each transaction as both a debit and a credit to make sure the records balanced.

This Italian coin was made to mark the 300th anniversary of Luca Pacioli's breakthrough.

860 Viking longships from Scandinavia sail as far west as Iceland, where Norwegians settle 14 years later.

866 The Vikings launch a fleet of up to 100 longships to invade England.

868 A Chinese printer creates the first printed book, a Buddhist work named *The Diamond Sutra.*

876 In Gwalior, India, people use a symbol for zero as a placeholder in a number system.

Shipbuilding

There were great advances in shipbuilding worldwide during medieval times. Ships were designed and built that could withstand powerful waves and sail across the world's oceans.

The war galleys and merchant vessels that had crossed the Mediterranean during the period of the Roman Empire were not at all suited to the rougher seas off northern Europe. There, bigger waves created more stress on the frame of a vessel, and galleys would break up under the pressure. A new way of building ships was devised by boat builders in Scandinavia. This involved making a hull where the planks overlapped and were not fitted edge to edge. A complete ship built using this so-called "clinker" method was found in Denmark and dated to 320 CE.

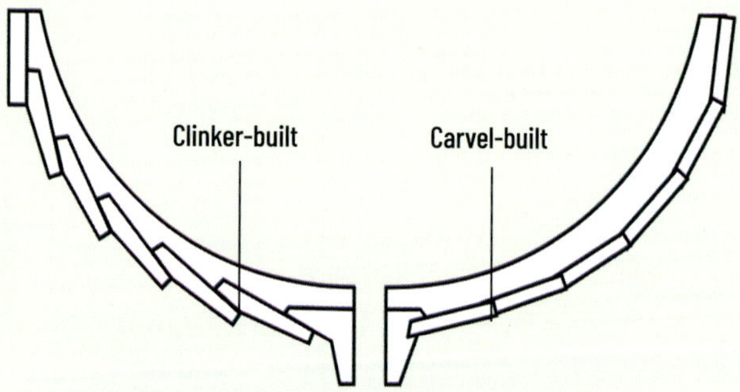

In clinker-built ships, the planks that make up the hull overlap each other. This makes the hull more flexible and watertight. Clinker building enabled the Vikings to make long voyages across stormy northern seas.

Clinker-built ships were flexible and could ride through the waves on stormy seas. The Vikings from Scandinavia used them to sail across the North Sea and out into the Atlantic, even reaching North

TIMELINE
880-950

KEY:

Life Sciences

Engineering and Technology

Astronomy and Math

880 Arab astronomer Abu-Abdullah Muhammad ibn-Jabir al-Battani (known in the West as Albategnius) introduces trigonometry to Arab astronomy; he corrects the work of Ptolemy, calculates the length of the year, and determines the precession of the equinoxes.

880

890

890 Mayan civilization in the southern lowlands is collapsing due to ecological problems.

America. These Viking ships used a single square sail if the wind was favorable. Otherwise, they could be powered by oarsmen.

Steering Merchant Vessels

Viking ships were steered by a single large oar mounted at the rear of the vessel. The next big European advance was the building of a type of ship known as the cog. These were large, clinker-built merchant vessels. From about 1200 onward, they were steered by a rudder mounted centrally at the stern, which was much more

Timeline

320 CE The date of the Nydam boat, the first known European vessel with a hull of overlapping planks (clinker-built)

790 The first Viking raid on England; the raiders used clinker-built longships to cross the North Sea

1200 First use of central rudders on cog merchant ships in northern Europe

1405 First voyage of Admiral Zheng He, who takes fleets of sea-going junks from China to explore southeast Asia and the Indian Ocean

1420 Portuguese sailors discover the island of Madeira in the Atlantic Ocean

A Viking war vessel, used for raiding. The vessel was so light it could be carried over land when necessary.

900 Persian-born Arab physician Rhazes distinguishes between the diseases measles and smallpox; he also uses plaster of Paris to hold broken bones as they heal.

900 Arab chemists distill wine to make alcohol, which they use mainly in medicine.

941 Otto I becomes the undisputed king of Germany and establishes an army based on heavily armored cavalry.

950 Arab settlers introduce the lemon plant to Sicily and Spain.

900 — 941 — 950

A map used by Zheng He during the planning of his voyages. West is at the top. Korea and Japan are marked, although they are clearly not to the correct scale.

efficient than the oar of the Viking longship. Because they were more efficient, cogs could be powered by a sail and barely used their oars.

Chinese Junks

Meanwhile, in China, a type of ship called a junk was being developed. Junks came in various shapes and sizes. Some were made from hardwood, such as teak, and some from softwood, such as pine. What they all had in common was a secure structure. The two sides of the hull were more or less parallel and the bottom of the ship was flat. Between the two parallel sides were strong bulkheads (walls) at 90 degrees to the sides, fixed in place with enormous nails. These bulkheads were watertight and made the vessel extremely seaworthy.

TIMELINE
954-976

KEY:

Engineering and Technology

Astronomy and Math

954 The Chinese emperor Shih Tsung commissions a huge statue of a lion; at 44 tons (40 metric tons), it is the largest piece of cast iron ever made in China.

954 960 964

960 In the Chinese province of Szechuan, paper money is printed and widely circulated as a means of exchange.

964 Arab astronomer Abd Al- Rahman Al-Sufi demonstrates the existence of the Andromeda Galaxy and the Large Magellanic Cloud.

Junks had sails made of linen or other cloth. These were kept in place by battens (bamboo strips). Some junks were very large, with up to 12 masts. They were steered by huge stern-mounted rudders that needed up to 20 men to control them. Admiral Zheng He took a fleet of these junks through the seas around China and across the Indian Ocean in a series of voyages from 1405 to 1433.

Dhows In the Indian Ocean, Zheng He's junk fleet would have come across another type of ocean-going vessel. These were dhows, handled by Arab sailors trading with India and down the east coast of Africa. The hulls were not nailed together but instead were sewn with tough ropes and cords. Although not very strong, these hulls were flexible. Dhows had triangular sails, which were much easier to manipulate than square sails and meant that dhows could use their sails for propulsion even when the wind was not directly behind them. The triangular, or lateen, sail gradually came into use in the Mediterranean from about 200 CE onwards. The complex skills involved in using

An Arab dhow, showing the lateen (triangular) sail that enables them to use the wind from many directions.

967 An iron pagoda for a Buddhist temple is cast in sections at Guangdong, China.

972 A university is founded in Cairo to study astronomy.

975 French cleric Gerbert of Aurillac builds a hydraulic musical organ.

976 A Chinese engineer invents a chain-drive mechanism for a mechanical clock.

lateen sails and the fact that the sails could put great pressure on the hull of a ship through the masts meant they were not widely adopted in northern Europe for many centuries.

Lateen sails were, however, used by Portuguese sailors who explored the Atlantic during the late Middle Ages. By 1431 they had reached the Azores and Madeira. Expeditions funded by the Portuguese prince known as Henry the Navigator then moved south along the west coast of Africa. Finally, in 1487, Bartholomew Diaz rounded the Cape of Good Hope into the Indian Ocean.

A caravel, with its lateen sails up. Such vessels enabled Portuguese sailors to explore the Atlantic Ocean and move down the west coast of Africa in the 15th century.

TIMELINE
981-1000

KEY:

Life Sciences

Engineering and Technology

Astronomy and Math

981 One of the world's first hospitals is built in the Abbasid capital at Baghdad; it employs 24 physicians.

982 Viking longships from Iceland cross the North Atlantic Ocean to discover Greenland.

984 A Chinese writer describes the first use of canal locks.

988 Persian astronomer Abu al- Wafa constructs a wall quadrant for observing the stars.

The carrack was a larger ship than a caravel. It had square sails and also a lateen rig toward the stern. Carracks were able to mount banks of guns and were developed into effective fighting warships during the 16th century.

Carvel Construction

The Portuguese sailors had small, maneuverable ships with lateen sails. These were called caravels, because they reverted to carvel construction. This is when the planks of the hull are set edge to edge rather than overlapping, giving the hull the strength to resist the pressures imposed through the masts by the lateen sails. Caravels were accompanied by larger vessels known as carracks, which were like a cross between a caravel and the northern European cog. These ships allowed the Portuguese and Spanish fleets to cross the Atlantic and Indian Oceans and establish the first European empires.

1000 Indian astronomers introduce a calendar with 360 days divided into 12 months; an extra month is inserted every five years to keep the calendar in step with the seasons.

1000

1000 Persian physician Avicenna writes *Canon of Medicine*, a standard medical textbook for centuries.

1000 The Chinese begin to use coal as a fuel; soon they begin to mine it.

Castles and Bridges

After the Norman Conquest of Britain in 1066, fortresses sprang up across the country. Castles and fortified bridges continued to be built in Europe until the 14th century.

The White Tower of the Tower of London was built by the Normans in 1080.

TIMELINE
1006-1045

KEY:

Engineering and Technology

Astronomy and Math

1006 1013 1021

1006 Astronomers around the world observe a supernova that remains visible for months.

1013 The al-Hakim mosque in Cairo is completed. It is one of the largest mosques so far constructed.

1021 Arab mathematician Alhazen publishes a treatise on optics in which he describes lenses and the refraction of light.

A castle is a fortified building. Originally, castles were constructed as strongholds for the kings or lords of the surrounding lands, and were designed to be as safe from attack as possible. As the techniques and weapons improved for assaulting and laying siege to castles, walls were made thicker and higher. Castles also became larger to accommodate all the people and supplies needed to manage and sustain them.

Motte-and-Bailey Castles

When the Normans invaded England in 1066, they constructed many new castles, using a style found elsewhere throughout western Europe. The stronghold (keep), built of stone or wood, sat on top of a high mound, or motte,

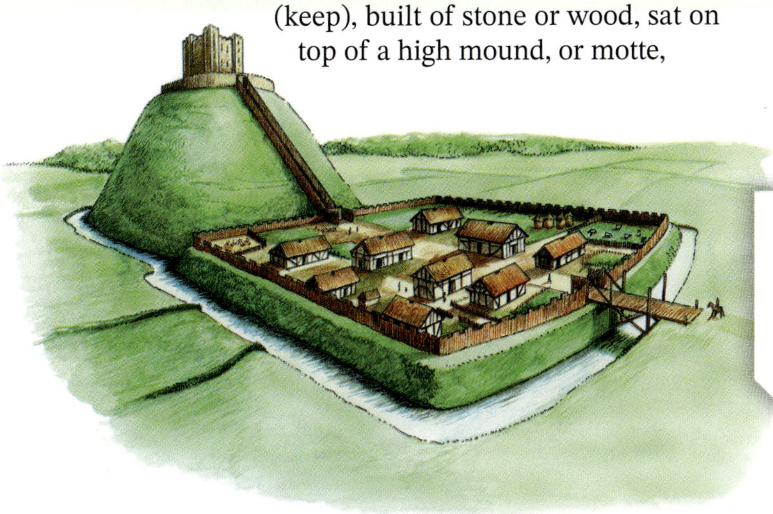

Motte-and-bailey castles had two parts. The motte was a mound with a wooden tower on top. The bailey lay at the foot of the hill, surrounded by a fence. It housed the ordinary people.

Timeline

1075 Round Tower of Windsor Castle

1080 White Tower (Tower of London)

1142 Knights of St. John in Krak des Chevaliers

1184 Avignon bridge

1198 Château Gaillard

1209 Old London Bridge

1322 Caernarfon Castle

1030 In Italy, the Benedictine monk Guido d'Arrezo invents the first form of musical notation (for writing down music).

1035 A hand-turned spinning wheel is introduced in China.

1044 A Chinese government official describes ballistic fire arrows, which are propelled by gunpowder.

1045 Movable type made from baked clay is invented for printing in China; it is credited to a cloth seller named Bi Sheng. Within a decade, the invention is used for printing books.

The Stone Keep

At the center of the castle lay the keep. This was the most heavily fortified part of any castle and was the place to which defenders retreated if an enemy broke through the outer walls. The keep held the owner's living quarters and stores. It had a well and could withstand a long siege. In later castles, residential quarters were often in the bailey, leaving the keep as the last line of defense.

The keep's high walls prevented attackers from scaling the battlements.

surrounded by a ditch. At its foot would be areas, called wards, that were protected by wooden palisades (fences made of stakes). This was known as a bailey, and so this is a motte-and-bailey type of castle.

The tall keep rises over Chepstow Castle, built on top of a sheer river cliff on the border between England and Wales.

Motte-and-bailey castles were used by the Normans in the early stages of their invasion of Britain. The artificial earthen mound in the center of Windsor Castle dates from about 1075. The Normans also built castles of stone. The rectangular White Tower at the Tower of London dates from 1080. Castle walls varied in thickness, depending on the degree to which they were exposed to attack. Most were 6–7 feet (1.8–2.1 m) thick.

TIMELINE
1050-1075

KEY:

Life Sciences

Engineering and Technology

Astronomy and Math

1050 Arab astronomers and navigators introduce the astrolabe into Europe.

1054 Astronomers in China and Japan record the sudden appearance of a supernova in the Crab Nebula that is visible in daylight for 23 days.

1066 What is later known as Halley's comet is sighted in England; it is interpreted as an omen of the Norman invasion of that year.

Building Baileys

One or more moats, sometimes with baileys between the moats, protected the castle's outer wall. Château Gaillard, on a cliff above the Seine River in France, has three baileys. The inner bailey is between the foot of the motte and the inner moat, a middle bailey between the inner moat and the outer walls, and an outer bailey outside the walls but protected by the outer moat. The three baileys are in line, so an invader would have to take all three before reaching the keep. Richard I of England built Château Gaillard between 1196 and 1198, and in its day it was one of the best-protected castles in Europe.

Drawbridges crossed the moats, and the gateways were often protected by walled structures (barbicans) outside the main castle wall. As the drawbridge was raised, a portcullis

Conwy Castle

Conwy Castle in Wales was built by English king Edward I as one of the key fortresses in his "iron ring," a series of strongholds built at key points to subdue the Welsh. Instead of having concentric walls within walls for defense, Conwy towered up from an enormous natural rock, so it was virtually impossible to attack. Its thick walls contained eight huge towers.

This illustration includes a cutaway showing the main hall of the castle, which was used for eating and for entertainment.

1075 In Toledo, Spain, Arab astronomer al-Zarqali builds complex astronomical water clocks.

1075

1075 In Italy, Trotula of Salerno works as an obstetrician, lectures at the university, and writes about female disorders—all unusual work for a woman at the time.

1075 Arab astronomer al-Zarqali, also known as Arzachel, proposes correctly that the orbits of the planets are elliptical rather than circular.

The Krak des Chevaliers

Built by Christian Crusaders in what is now Syria, the Krak des Chevaliers is one of the most impressive medieval fortresses. Perched on a mountain spur that drops away on three sides, it occupied a strong defensive position. Its entrance was guarded by a complex series of twists and turns. The castle remained impregnable for nearly 130 years after it was built.

The Krak des Chevaliers in Syria was built to defend Crusaders against local people.

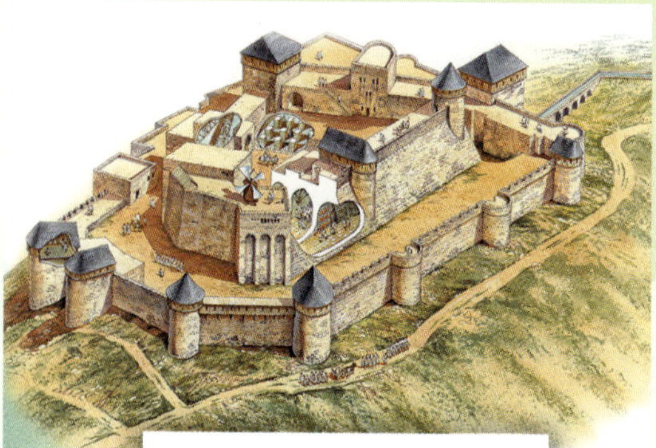

Krak des Chevaliers had two widely spaced walls to reinforce its hilltop position.

(a screen made of wood and iron) could be lowered so that it closed off the gateway completely.

A castle displayed the wealth and power of its owner. After the English king Edward I suppressed the Welsh in 1282–1283, he built six castles to house his garrisons and to remind local people of his power. Caernarfon Castle, built between 1283 and 1322, is still standing today.

The Crusaders of the Middle Ages built many castles, one of the most impressive being the strategically located Krak des Chevaliers

TIMELINE
1080-1103

KEY:

Life Sciences

Engineering and Technology

Astronomy and Math

1080 European farmers use the "swingletree" to allow two horses to pull a wagon or plow side by side.

1086 Shen Kua discusses earth science, including the principles of sedimentation, uplift, and erosion.

1080

1086

1086 One of the first attempts in northern Europe to quantify the population and wealth of country by a census is started in England. It is called the *Domesday Book*.

1086 Chinese scientist Shen Kua describes a magnetic compass used for navigation.

(castle of the knights) at Qal 'at al-Hisn, Syria. With an inner and outer wall separated by a wide ditch, it could hold a garrison of 2,000 soldiers. The Knights of St. John (the Knights Hospitallers) built the castle and held it from 1142 until Sultan Baybars I captured it in 1271.

Decline of Castles

Although castles were strong, they were not able to resist the gunpowder weapons that came into use from 1350 onward. In the end, guns were powerful enough to reduce walls to rubble. The importance of castles waned, and lords built comfortable palaces instead.

Fortified Bridges of Europe

Bridges are such key defensive points that some, such as the 14th-century Pont Valentré at Cahors, southern France, were fortified. The bridge had three towers so defenders could keep traffic from crossing. Other important bridges had shops, chapels, and other buildings all the way across. Old London Bridge was the first bridge with masonry foundations built on a swift-flowing tidal river—the Thames. Lined with houses and shops, it survived for more than 600 years.

With three fortified towers, the Pont Valentré spans the Lot River in southern France.

1090 A Chinese minister builds a larger water-driven astronomical clock called the "Cosmic Engine."

1100 After the invention of gunpowder, colorful fireworks become popular in China.

1103 Chinese potters make a fine white ceramic called porcelain, which in Europe is called "china."

Chinese Science

Some of the world's greatest inventions originated in China. Early Chinese scientists invented the kite, spinning wheel, compass, crossbow, and wheelbarrow.

The Chinese enjoyed fireworks displays over 1,000 years ago.

TIMELINE
1105-1140

KEY:

Life Sciences

Engineering and Technology

Astronomy and Math

1105 Persian mathematician and poet Omar Khayyam solves cubic equations (algebra equations of the degree 3).

1110 European military engineers invent the gravity-powered trebuchet.

1120 Prior Walcher of Malvern Abbey, England, begins using degrees to express latitude and longitude on maps.

1125 In Toledo, Spain, craftsmen are producing high-quality swords by combining two different types of steel.

Chinese general Meng T'ien is credited with inventing the camel's-hair brush as a tool for writing in 250 BCE. In those days, people wrote on cloth, but the popularity of the brush led to a demand for a cheaper and more plentiful medium. In about 105 CE, Ts'ai Lun invented paper. The oldest-known printed book (a Chinese translation of the *Diamond Sutra*, a Buddhist text) is also Chinese, made in 868 CE.

Chinese books on alchemy, also from the ninth century, contain formulas for making mixtures that burn with a flash: early gunpowder. In 132 CE a scholar, Chang Heng, invented an "earthquake weathercock." In fact, it was a seismograph.

Timeline

1000 BCE Kite

600 BCE Iron plowshare

250 BCE Camel's-hair brush

1st century CE Rudder

100 CE Wheelbarrow

c.105 Paper

132 Seismograph

868 First printed book

Chinese Thought

Chinese and European thought developed along very different lines. Chinese thinkers had no key philosophical ideas, or theology. Each science was separate and produced partial and often indirect explanations for natural patterns and relationships that scholars believed were too complex to be fully understood.

This Chinese compass used a lodestone (natural magnet) to indicate north and south.

Astronomy was very important because the Chinese believed the emperor must preserve a harmonious relationship with the

1126 Chinese military forces use gunpowder rockets and grenades in the defense of Kaifeng.

1140 King Roger II of Sicily introduces a system of government licenses that enable physicians to practice medicine.

1126 1135 1140

1135 Scholars in Toledo, Spain, translate the medical works of Persian physician and philosopher Avicenna into Latin.

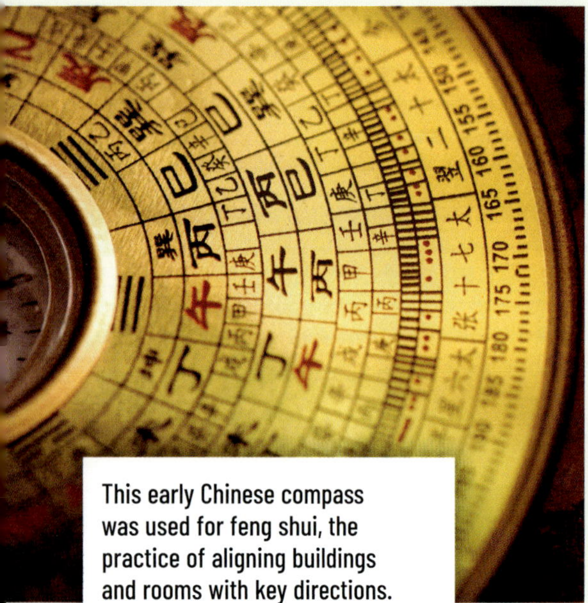

This early Chinese compass was used for feng shui, the practice of aligning buildings and rooms with key directions. It was only later that the compass was used for navigation.

cosmic order by living a pure and simple life and correctly performing rituals. This required a reliable calendar, based on astronomical observations.

The present Chinese calendar emerged in the 14th century. The calendar counted days, months, and years in cycles of 60. As well as marking the equinoxes, solstices, and agricultural seasons, the Chinese calendar contained the dates of predictable events. Irregular and unpredictable events were seen as omens. Chinese astronomers kept detailed records. From as early as the fourth century BCE, they noted the positions of stars in star tables, and there is a continuous record from about 70 BCE.

Chinese Math

Astronomy is a mathematical science, and the earliest-known Chinese mathematical text is the *Zhoubi Suanjing (Zhou Dynasty Canon of Gnomic Computations)*, written sometime between 400 and 200 BCE but based on much earlier texts, now lost.

Early Chinese mathematicians noticed the relationship between a sound's pitch and the physical processes that produce it. This led to Chinese harmonics (used to tune stone chimes and bells used in rituals)

TIMELINE
1140-1155

KEY:

Life Sciences

Engineering and Technology

Astronomy and Math

1140 Construction of a new basilica at the Abbey of Saint Denis begins in France; the building has a new form of supporting columns named flying buttresses.

1140

1150

1150 The first papermill in Europe is built in Valencia, Spain.

The wheelbarrow appeared in China in about 100 CE for transporting goods.

and then to the development of court music. In 1978, archaeologists discovered 65 bronze bells with gold-inlaid inscriptions in a tomb from the fifth century BCE.

Chinese Medicine

Chinese medicine was based on the cosmic principles of yin and yang. These were seemingly conflicting patterns or forces that could actually be reconciled. It began about 2953 BCE. Much of Chinese medical literature is based on the text *Nei Ching*, traditionally attributed to the legendary Yellow Emperor, but probably written in the third century BCE. Doctors relied on the use of herbal, animal, and mineral substances. They used massage, physical and breathing exercises, and diet. The studies covered thousands of ingredients, increasing the Chinese people's knowledge of natural history.

The Crossbow

Crossbows were in use in China by the sixth century BCE. While conventional bows relied on the strength of the archer, the crossbow had a trigger, so that many bolts could be fired in quick succession without tiring the user. The greater tension on a crossbow string than on a conventional bow string makes the bolt travel farther and penetrate even thick armor. The trigger also gave the crossbow great accuracy over a long range.

Chinese emperors had thousands of crossbow archers in their armies.

1150 In Spain, Arab physician Avenzoar introduces bloodletting as a medical treatment.

1155 The oldest-known printed maps are created in China, showing the west of the country.

1150

1155

1150 Indian knowledge of algebra and arithmetic are summed up in *Siddhanta Siromani*.

1150 Hebrew astronomer Solomon Jarchus compiles the first celestial almanac, giving details about the stars.

Medieval Warfare

War was the driving force behind many technological advances during the Middle Ages. Military technology included better steel blades for swords, and massive siege machines using the counterweight principle.

Perhaps the most important technological advance during warfare in the Middle Ages was the invention of the stirrup. Stirrups gave a warrior on horseback much greater stability than before. Without stirrups, a cavalry soldier could not swing a heavy weapon, such as an ax, downward without the risk of falling off his mount. With stirrups as support, cavalry soldiers became extremely effective across Asia and Europe during the medieval period.

No one knows for sure who invented the stirrup. Stirrups have to be fixed to a solid saddle in order to spread the weight of the rider across the back of the horse. If the saddle is not made properly, chafing

Cavalrymen using heavy weapons against infantry. In the ancient world, cavalry could not use long swords and other weapons while mounted on horseback.

TIMELINE
1175-1200

KEY:

Life Sciences

Engineering and Technology

Astronomy and Math

1175 In Italy, Gerard of Cremona translates the *Almagest* of Greek astronomer Ptolemy from Arabic into Latin.

1180 European shipbuilders begin making ships steered by a rudder rather than by steering oars.

1175

1180

1180 Italian physician Roger of Salerno publishes *Practice of Surgery*, the first European book dedicated to surgery.

and pain makes the horse difficult to manage and shortens its working life. Drawings of loops that resemble stirrups were first seen in the early centuries CE, but they were probably aids to mounting the horse rather than aids to riding. A Chinese tomb dating to 322 CE contains a pair of stirrups. From that time onward the use of stirrups spread across the Eurasian steppes, and by the 700s stirrups were in use in Europe.

Chain Mail

Stirrups led on for other advances in medieval weaponry. The security of stirrups meant that cavalrymen could now wear heavier armor than before and carry weapons such as the long broadsword. The armor could be heavier than the armor that a foot soldier would wear. In Europe, heavy chain tunics (called hauberks) were made from rings of iron. Iron was heated and pulled out into thin

Timeline

322 CE A pair of stirrups found in a tomb near Nanjing

947 Crossbows used as weapons by French troops at the siege of Senlis

1200 Trebuchets, siege weapons using the counterweight principle to throw projectiles used in Europe

1246 Battle of Legnica. Mongol horse archers with composite bows defeat army of heavily armored European knights

1346 Gunpowder weapons used in Europe at the battle of Crécy

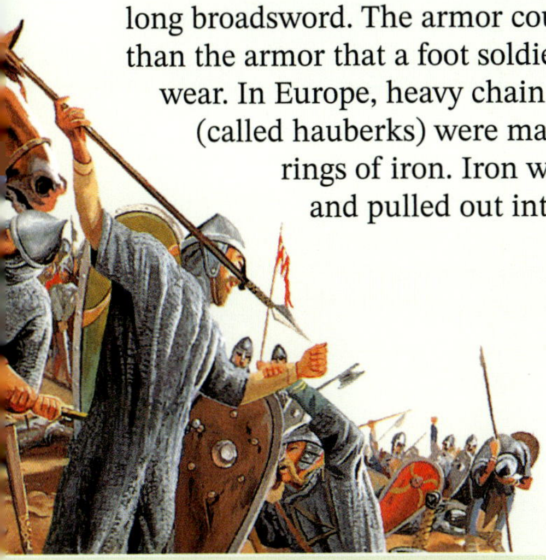

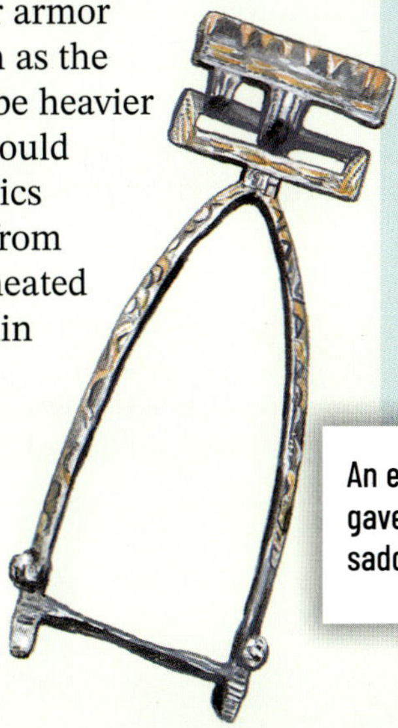

An early European stirrup. The stirrup gave cavalrymen security in the saddle when using their weapons.

1181 Chinese and Japanese astronomers describe a supernova that can be seen for over six months.

1185 Chinese jade workers invent the rotary disk cutter to cut jadestone.

1193 Italian scholar Burgundio of Pisa translates the works of the Greek physician Galen into Latin; they have a huge influence on medicine for the following centuries.

1200 Chinese mathematicians introduce a symbol for zero.

1181 1185 1193 1200

wires that could be bent into rings and linked together. In the best chain mail, each ring was linked to four others. This was skilled work that needed precision and a good understanding of metal working in order to make the wires the right diameter.

Plate Armor

Expert metal craftsmen began creating solid plates of armor as an even more effective protection for cavalrymen. These plates were lighter than chain mail, and by the 15th century complete suits of armor were made that covered the body entirely. Armor was also made to protect the horses.

The technology of using iron and steel (iron made harder by the addition of small amounts of carbon), was also developed by craftsmen making swords. The key to making sharper, stronger swords was to control the amount of carbon in the steel. The best sword-making

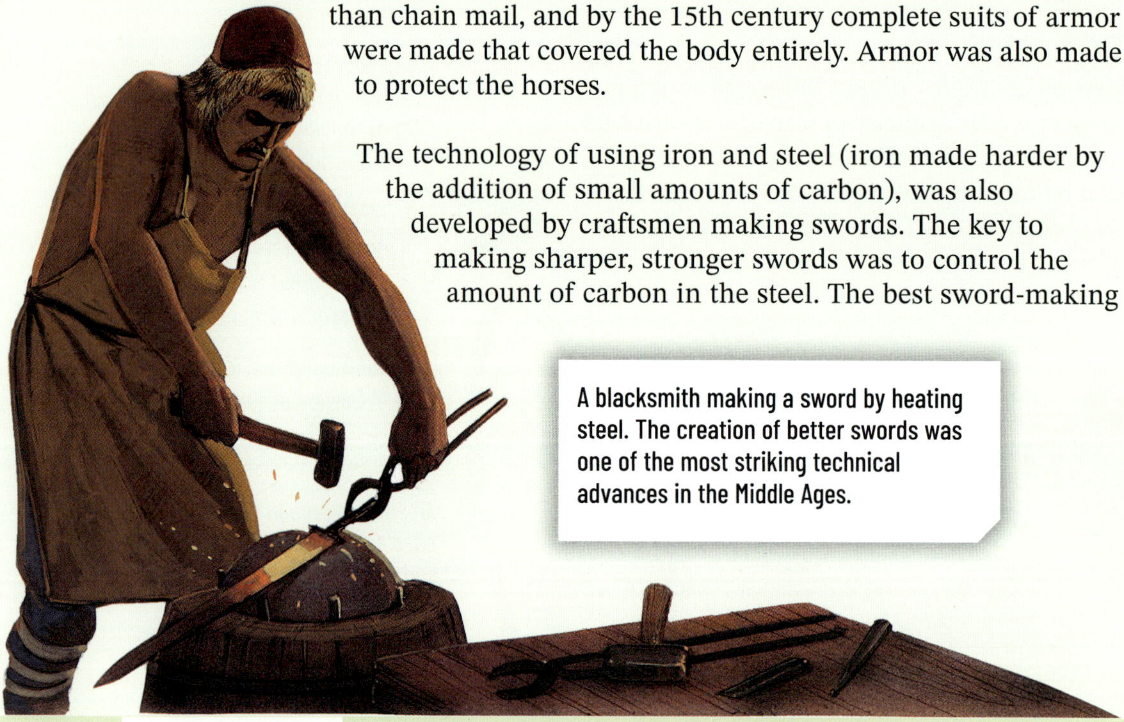

A blacksmith making a sword by heating steel. The creation of better swords was one of the most striking technical advances in the Middle Ages.

TIMELINE
1202-1227

KEY:
Life Sciences
Engineering and Technology
Astronomy and Math

1202

1202 Italian mathematician Leonardo Fibonacci introduces the Fibonacci series, a succession of numbers in which each number is the sum of the previous two.

1205

1205 European farmers begin to grow buckwheat as an alternative cereal crop.

1205 In Spain, ironworkers improve the Catalan forge, a forerunner of the blast furnace.

A piece of chain mail. Creating a chain mail tunic (hauberk) required great expertise.

centers were Toledo in Spain and Damascus in Syria. In Toledo, the swordsmiths devised a technique that was kept secret for centuries. They used two types of steel, each containing different amounts of carbon. One was soft for flexibility and one was harder to give the blade a sharp edge. The long process involved heating and cooling the two parts. It was said that even the most skilled swordsmith in Toledo could only produce three swords per year.

A knight and his horse in protective plate armor. Making such a suit of armor required months, if not years, of work by skilled craftsmen.

1217 Scottish scholar Michael Scot introduces the ideas of the ancient Greek scientist Aristotle into European astronomy.

1220 Universities are founded around now in Padua, Naples, Toulouse, Cambridge, and Rome.

1225 Drawings of a water-powered saw for cutting timber are made in France.

1227 Japanese artist Kato Shirozaemon uses Chinese technology to start producing fine china in Japan.

A crossbowman winching his bow into a firing position. Crossbows had great power, but were slow to load on the battlefield.

The longbow and arrowlike projectiles had been an important weapon in the ancient world. During the Middle Ages, many armies still used the simple one-piece bow that was drawn back to the nose or the ear. But although these could be effective, they relied on great physical strength to hold the bow steady while aiming and firing. The crossbow had been invented in China, and it meant that an archer could aim at a target while resting his weapon on a support before pulling a trigger to release the bolt. This was a more accurate weapon. The crossbow was also more powerful than the longbow. The addition of a stirrup and a winding mechanism made it easier to pull the bowstring back to load the crossbow.

Composite Bows

Perhaps the most effective bows in use during the Middle Ages were those of the Middle East and the Eurasian steppes. These bows were made with a core of wood, but with a section of horn glued to the central section facing the archer. Animal sinews were glued to the outside. When the bowstring was drawn, the horn became compressed and the sinews stretched. Both of these added force to the arrow as it sped away toward its target. In the hands of the Mongol armies under Genghis Khan, these bows proved devastating.

TIMELINE
1240-1250

KEY:

Life Sciences

Engineering and Technology

Astronomy and Math

1240

1240 A decree of the Holy Roman Empire permits the dissection of human corpses.

1240 English mathematician Johannes de Sacrobosco publishes *On the Sphere of the World*, a standard astronomical text for four centuries.

1240 Arab physician Ibn al-Baytar lists 1,400 medications in a catalog of medicines and foodstuffs.

Siege Warfare

Much of medieval warfare was not concerned with open battles, but with siege warfare. This was the taking and holding of castles, cities, or towns. The Roman army had used weapons that used forces of tension (as in pulling back a bowstring) and torsion (the force of twisted ropes). In the Middle Ages, inventors came up with machines that used an even more effective force—the counterweight. From about 1200, machines called trebuchets were in use in Europe, having first been used in China. The best trebuchets were like seesaws, long poles balanced on a fulcrum. A box of heavy stones was placed on the shorter end of the arm. The other end was held down and had a sling tied to it that contained a single stone. When the sling end was released, the heavy weights in the box shot the long arm up and the stone was hurled out of the sling with great velocity.

A trebuchet, the most powerful medieval siege engine until gunpowder became the weapon of choice.

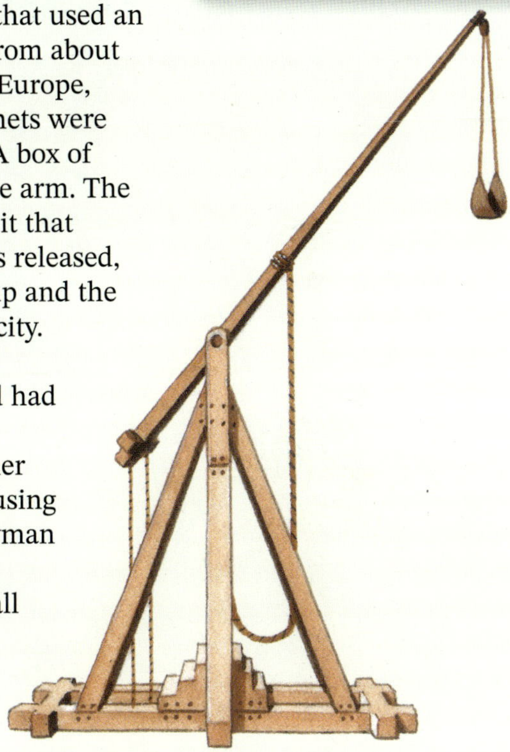

Many weapons developed in the medieval period had originally come from China. What transformed warfare at the end of the Middle Ages was another Chinese invention: gunpowder. When weapons using gunpowder were developed, the armored cavalryman gradually became less strategically important in warfare. Siege warfare, too, was changed out of all recognition. High stone walls could now be destroyed by cannon firing heavy stones or deadly metal projectiles.

1242 English philosopher Roger Bacon gives precise instructions on how to make gunpowder.

1250 German monk Albertus Magnus isolates arsenic.

1242 1250 1255

1250 Armorers in Bohemia (in what is now the Czech Republic) make armor with tinplate, which does not rust.

1255 Carrier pigeons are used to carry messages in the Middle East—up to 400 miles (640 km) a day.

The Magnetic Compass

The development of the magnetic compass has its roots in China. Later, in Europe, the compass became more sophisticated and an essential tool for exploration.

The magnetic compass was essential for navigation in the age of exploration.

TIMELINE
1261–1286

KEY:

Life Sciences

Engineering and Technology

Astronomy and Math

1261

1262

1262 Arab astronomer Nasir al- Din al-Tusi builds a well-equipped astronomical observatory at Maragheh, in present-day Iraq.

1261 In China, what is now called the Marco Polo bridge has become a major route for traffic across the Yongding River. Constructed 50 years previously, it is 770 feet (235 m) long and based on 10 piers and 11 arches.

The history of the compass and that of magnetism are closely linked. People knew about magnetism thousands of years ago, when they saw the unusual properties of certain rocks called lodestones, which are rich in magnetite, a mixed iron oxide (Fe_3O_4), that is naturally magnetic. A shepherd named Magnus (magnet) discovered lodestones when he noticed that the iron tip of his crook stuck to certain rocks.

Magnets and Navigation

Earth is a giant magnet. Its magnetic field is generated by electrical currents and convection currents in Earth's outer core. Earth's magnetic field has two poles: north and south. By the first century CE, lodestones were used in devices called south-pointers, used by Chinese mystics for astrology and fortune-telling. During the eighth century, the lodestone in Chinese compasses was replaced by a magnetized iron needle. In 1086, Chinese scientist Shen Kua described a magnetic compass used for navigation. In 1117, Chu Yu's P'ingchow described the use of a compass at sea. But it was not until the age of European exploration that the device became a sophisticated navigational aid.

Timeline

1st century CE South-pointers (lodestones)

8th century Iron compass needles

11th century Vikings believed to use compasses at sea

1250 European sailors use portable compasses

1269 Compass dial

The Chinese used compasses to align buildings in order to achieve positive energies.

1269 French writer Petrus Peregrinus introduces the idea that a magnet has "poles" at either end.

1272 *The Alfonsine Tables*, the first astronomical tables prepared in Christian Europe, are published after 10 years' work.

1276 In China, Zhou Kung builds a 40-foot (12m) shadow clock.

1276 Italian physician Giles of Rome discusses the role each parent plays in reproduction.

1286 Eyeglasses are invented in Italy at about this time.

Magnetic Deviation

Earth's magnetic north and south poles are not aligned with the true poles (the axis on which the planet spins). The effect is greater the closer you are to the poles. Things are complicated by the fact that Earth's magnetic field is not static. The positions of magnetic north and south drift slightly over time. But the movement is gradual, and can be easily compensated for when using a compass to give true directions.

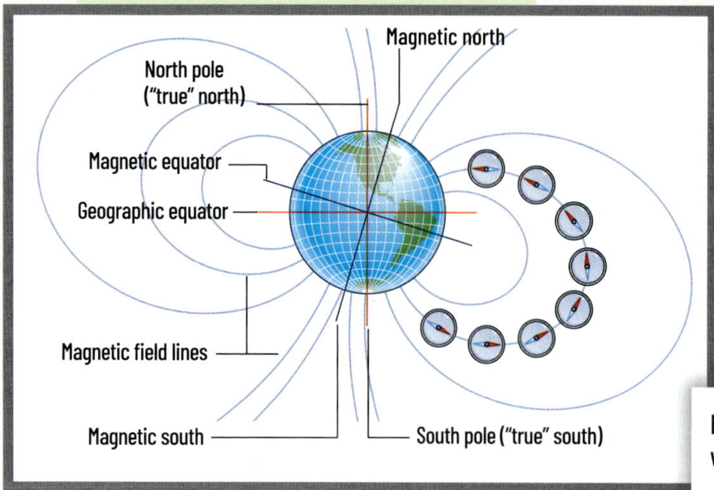

Earth has its own magnetic field, which causes magnetic deviation.

It was probably the Arabs who brought the compass to the West. Before that, European travelers used the sun or the polestar to show them north and south. They could achieve remarkable accuracy, but only with clear skies. Periods of bad weather made such navigation impossible, often with deadly, catastrophic results.

The Compass in Europe

The Vikings may have used compasses in the 11th century, but the first written reference to a magnetic compass in the West comes from *De Naturis Rerum (Concerning Natural Things)*, published around 1180 by English scholar Alexander Neckam.

Early European compasses were not convenient for travel. By 1250, a needle was mounted on a pivot so that it hovered beneath a circular card marked up with the cardinal directions.

TIMELINE
1290–1320

KEY:

Life Sciences

Engineering and Technology

Astronomy and Math

1290 In the Andes, people build cable bridges across deep gorges.

1300 False Gerber, a Spanish alchemist, first prepares sulfuric acid.

1304 German scientist Theodoric of Freiberg investigates how raindrops form rainbows and discovers that refraction causes a colored spectrum.

When the needle moved, so did the card. A French scientist and soldier, Petrus Peregrinus, first described the laws governing the behavior of magnets (and hence of the compass) in 1269. He described magnetic poles and developed a compass dial, which allowed greater accuracy.

In this mariner's compass, the needle hovers from a pivot just below the dial, and the whole instrument is set inside a sturdy case that could be mounted on gimbals to keep it steady at sea.

Further refinements followed, including mounting the needle and dial inside a box made of wood or ivory, materials that did not interfere with the magnetic forces. Later models used brass for the same reason. In the 16th century, ships' compasses began to be mounted on self-correcting bearings, or "gimbals," that ensured the compass was always level despite the rolling of the ship.

An Indispensable Tool

Compasses became indispensable. In 1594, English philosopher Francis Bacon described the "needle" as one of the three most important advancements in the civilized world (the others being gunpowder and the printing press). As time went by, navigators realized that the compass needle was not infallible. It could be deflected by the proximity of certain objects, especially those made of iron. At sea, compasses could also be influenced by large landmasses; and when traveling east or west, navigators had to compensate for a phenomenon known as magnetic deviation.

1305 1310 1313 1316 1320

1305 The hourglass is invented for telling the time.

1310 Portuguese sailors begin to make and use portolan charts to help with coastal navigation.

1313 *Noww Shu*, a book on agriculture, is printed by Chinese printer Wang Chen. He uses 50,000 characters made from hardwood rather than the clay characters previously in use.

1316 Italian anatomist Mondino De' Luzzi publishes the first Western account of anatomy.

1320 French surgeon Henri de Mondeville recommends the cleansing and stitching of wounds to aid healing.

Alchemists

In the medieval period, alchemists were thinkers who believed they could change the natures of matter. Although their attempts failed, some of them made useful discoveries.

During the late Roman Empire, people who thought about and studied the world around them were known as natural philosophers. Most of them believed that all matter was created from a mixture of four substances. These were fire (hot and dry), earth (cold and dry), water (cold and moist), and air (hot and moist).

Some people in the ancient world thought that matter could be changed by altering the balance of these four substances in a material. However, no detailed accounts have survived from this period. After the creation of a large Islamic empire that covered much of the Middle East and North Africa, Islamic scholars began to look at such ideas, and developed them further. The most important scholar was Jabir ibn Hayyan (721–815 CE), later known in Europe as Geber. He thought there were eight core elements, and that if these were changed, the nature of metals could be altered. For this change to take place, a new substance needed to be added to the metal. He called this substance al-iksir ("elixir" in English).

Jabir ibn Hayyan, the Islamic scholar who wrote extensively on alchemy and how to change the nature of metals.

TIMELINE
1325-1345

KEY:

Life Sciences

Engineering and Technology

Astronomy and Math

1325 The Hohokam people start building Casa Grande in what is now Arizona.

1330 French Hebrew mathematician Levi ben Gershom invents the cross-staff, used as a navigational aid.

1333 Europe's first medieval botanical gardens is opened in Venice, Italy.

This illustration from a 15th century manuscript shows an alchemist at work. A dragon eating its own tail is inside the flask set above a fire. A mythical bird, a phoenix, stands with outstretched wings. The bird was said to come back to life in fire.

Timeline

c.300 CE Zosimos of Panopolis describes alchemical experiments using mercury and sulfur, and how substances such as copper can be altered

c.815 Death of Jabir ibn Hayyan (Geber), author of various works on alchemy and eight core elements

1144 Robert of Chester translates a key Islamic alchemical text by Khalid ibn Yazid

1564 Englishman John Dee publishes the alchemical work *Monas Hieroglyphica*

1750 Alchemy is widely seen as being fraudulent practice designed to exploit the over-trusting people

The Philosopher's Stone

Geber's ideas were heavily criticized in the Muslim world, especially by later thinkers such as Avicenna. However, in Europe Geber's ideas spread widely. In about 1144, a text on alchemy by Khalid ibn Yazid was translated by Robert of Chester, an English scholar of Arabic texts. Western alchemists began to search for a substance that could transform metals. This elixir became known as the Philosopher's Stone. The great attraction of alchemy was that it promised to allow its practitioners to turn common, base metals (such as

1335 | 1336 | 1340 | 1345

1335 Andean cultures build bridges across Andean gorges using cables and ropes.

1336 Math becomes compulsory for all students at the University of Paris.

1340 The English start using avoirdupois weights (pounds and ounces), first used in France.

1345 Dutch engineers use windmills to pump water from low-lying land.

copper, tin, or zinc) into precious metals, such as gold and silver. The rewards of success would have been so great that alchemists kept their experiments secret. They tried heating and mixing different substances and metals. They also believed that magic would lead them to the Philosopher's Stone. Many late medieval scholars claimed to have made progress in finding the Philosopher's Stone. One was the German monk Albertus Magnus (c.1200-1280), although he never claimed to have discovered it. He did, however, conduct experiments that led to the isolation of arsenic by heating soap with arsenic trisulfide.

The Polish scientist Michael Sendivogius (1566–1636). It is thought that his experiments in search of the Philosopher's Stone led to the later discovery of oxygen.

TIMELINE
1346-1364

KEY:

Life Sciences

Engineering and Technology

Astronomy and Math

1346 The "Black Death" arrives in Europe; within four years it kills about a quarter of the population: 25 million people.

1350 Ironfounders in Liege, Belgium, make a blast furnace for extracting iron from its ore.

1350 Muslim architects adopt a style of building mosques based on four vaulted halls around a courtyard.

This painting by Joseph Wright of Derby (1734–1797) is titled *The Alchemist Discovering Phosphorus* or *The Alchemist in Search of The Philosopher's Stone.*

Later Alchemy

During the 16th and 17th centuries, many European rulers invested in the experiments of alchemists, hoping to gain great riches. Some alchemists, such as Michael Sendivogius (1566–1636) did succeed in making discoveries that were useful for later scientists. People now considered to be modern scientists, such as Isaac Newton, also devoted much of their time to alchemy. However, by the late-18th century, alchemy and the search for the Philosopher's Stone was increasingly abandoned in favor of more modern methods.

1353 1355 1363 1364

1353 Gunpowder weapons used by English armies invading France during the Hundred Years' War.

1355 French philosopher Jean Buridan comes up with the idea of "impetus," which keeps celestial bodies continuously in orbit.

1363 French physician Guy de Chauliac describes how to treat fractures and hernias.

1364 Italian clockmaker Giovanni di Dondi makes an astronomical clock.

Clocks and Watches

The earliest timekeeper, used in ancient Egypt by about 3500 BCE, was a vertical stick in the ground that showed the time by the position of its shadow as the sun moved.

This 24-hour clock at the Capitano Palace in Padua, Italy, was built in 1344.

TIMELINE

1377–1395

KEY:

Life Sciences

Engineering and Technology

Astronomy and Math

1377 1379 1380

1377 Authorities at what is now Dubrovnik in Croatia use an island to quarantine travelers as a defense against the plague.

1379 Italian writer Gabriel de Lavinde publishes a treatise on codes, which were in common use at the time (especially for diplomatic correspondence).

1380 Inca officials in South America use knotted strings known as quipu to keep records of goods and taxes.

By the eighth century BCE, the shadow clock had evolved into the sundial, with a triangular "fin" replacing the stick. Sand clocks also date from ancient times. The most common type, developed in the 14th century, was the hourglass, so called because it took one hour for dry sand to run from the upper section to the lower section. The British Royal Navy used hourglasses on board ships at sea until the 1820s.

Other Devices

At night, when sundials naturally did not work, the ancient Egyptians used water clocks (clepsydra) to tell the time. The simplest water clock consisted of a vessel full of water with a graduated scale marked on the inside. As water dripped out of the vessel through a hole in the bottom, the level on the scale inside showed the time. The Greeks added a float mechanism to move a pointer toward the time. Chinese inventors used mercury and water in their versions of a clepsydra.

In 725 CE, Chinese engineer Liang Ling-Zan and Buddhist monk Yi-Xing made the first mechanical clock, based on the movement of a huge 33-foot (10-m) paddlewheel. Each "paddle" was a cup that filled with water and rotated the wheel by exactly one-thirty-sixth of a turn. In about 1090, Chinese imperial minister Su Sung built a huge water-driven astronomical clock, or

Timeline

725 First mechanical water-driven clock

996 Clock escapement

1380s Weight-driven clocks

1502 Spring-driven clock

1656 First pendulum clock

1675 Hairspring regulator

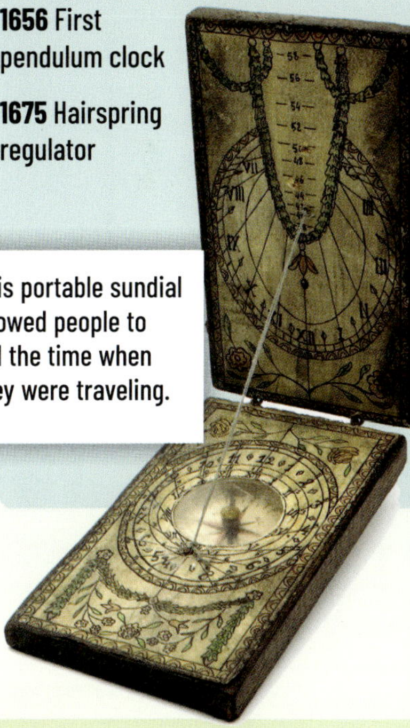

This portable sundial allowed people to tell the time when they were traveling.

1380 Military rockets are used in Europe for the first time at the Battle of Chioggia, between Genoese and Venetian armies.

1391 The poet Geoffrey Chaucer writes the first technology book in English; it includes a description of a sextant.

1395 Printers in Korea use metal type.

1395 Chinese astronomers calculate the length of the solar year as 365.25 days (today's most accurate measurement is 365.242 days).

Verge-and-Foliot Escapement

In a verge-and-foliot escapement, the verge was controlled by teeth (pallets) that engaged a crown wheel. As the foliot swung, a pallet disengaged the crown wheel, allowing the weight to fall and turn the hand. The foliot swung back, and a pallet engaged the crown wheel, stopping the fall of the weight. The foliot then swung in the other direction, allowing the weight to fall once again.

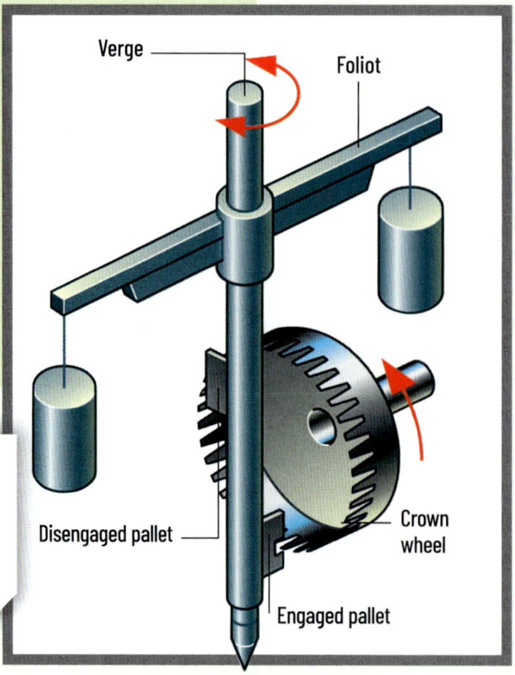

The verge-and-foliot escapement was used to regulate clocks until about 1800.

"Cosmic Engine," which showed the apparent movement of the stars through the sky as well as the time.

The Mechanical Clock

The first mechanical clocks were driven by the action of a slowly falling weight at the end of a cord wrapped around a drum. Every hour, a hammer rang a bell (there were no hands or dials). "Clock" comes from the German *glock*, meaning bell. This type of clock was invented by the French cleric and scholar Gerbert of Aurillac in about 996. Similar clocks dating from the 1380s still exist in cathedrals in France and England.

In 1502, German clockmaker Peter Henlein invented a spring-driven clock with a horizontal face and a single hour

TIMELINE
1400–1425

KEY:
Life Sciences
Engineering and Technology
Astronomy and Math

1400 Dutch and Flemish artists begin to use oil-based paints.

1405 Triangular lateen sails are used by Spanish sailors; they spread throughout the Mediterranean region.

1410 Hebrew astronomer Hasdai ben Abraham Crescas disagrees with Aristotle's theory that there are no other worlds except Earth.

1410 People in Ethiopia make coffee from the berries of the wild coffee plant.

hand. In 1656, Christiaan Huygens, a Dutch scientist, designed the pendulum clock. The first one was made a year later by Salomon Coster in the Hague. English scientist Robert Hooke invented the anchor escapement in 1660. This allowed the clock to release its energy gradually and regularly.

Watches

Henlein also made the first portable timekeeper, or watch, shortly before he died in 1542. Spring-driven, it had an hour hand that showed through holes in the case. The oscillating balance wheel and hairspring regulator were invented in about 1675; they are still used today. Then, in 1680, English clockmaker Daniel Quare invented a pocket watch that chimed the hours.

Anchor Escapement

The anchor escapement was used in long-case clocks from about 1670. The swinging pendulum causes a horseshoe-shaped anchor to rock from side to side. The rocking motion allows the escape wheel to make a fraction of a turn at each half-swing. This action allows the driving weight to fall very slowly, rotating the barrel and so turning the hands of the clock.

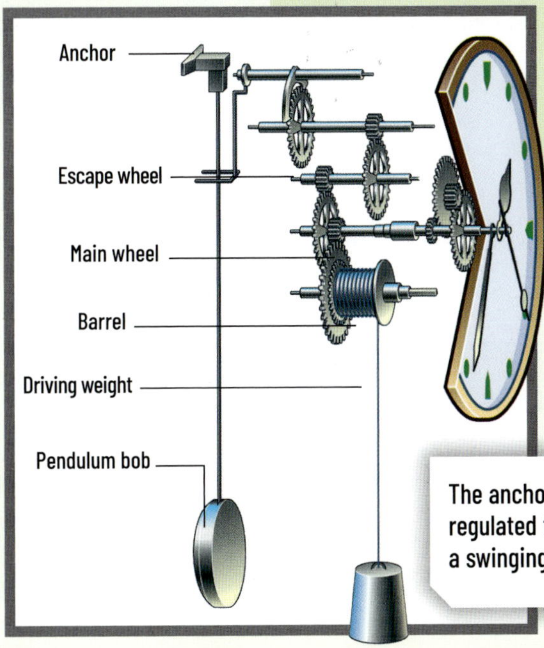

The anchor escapement regulated the action of a swinging pendulum.

1414 Fleets of large, oceangoing junks begin sailing from China to India, the Middle East, and as far as Africa.

1420 Filippo Brunelleschi begins building the dome of Florence Cathedral in Italy.

1425 German cleric Nicholas of Cusa suggests that Earth rotates on its axis every day and orbits the sun once a year; he anticipates by 100 years the similar theories of Polish astronomer Nicolaus Copernicus.

Guns and Gunpowder

Gunpowder is a Chinese invention from the 11th century. The black powder and the firearms that used it changed the course of history across the globe.

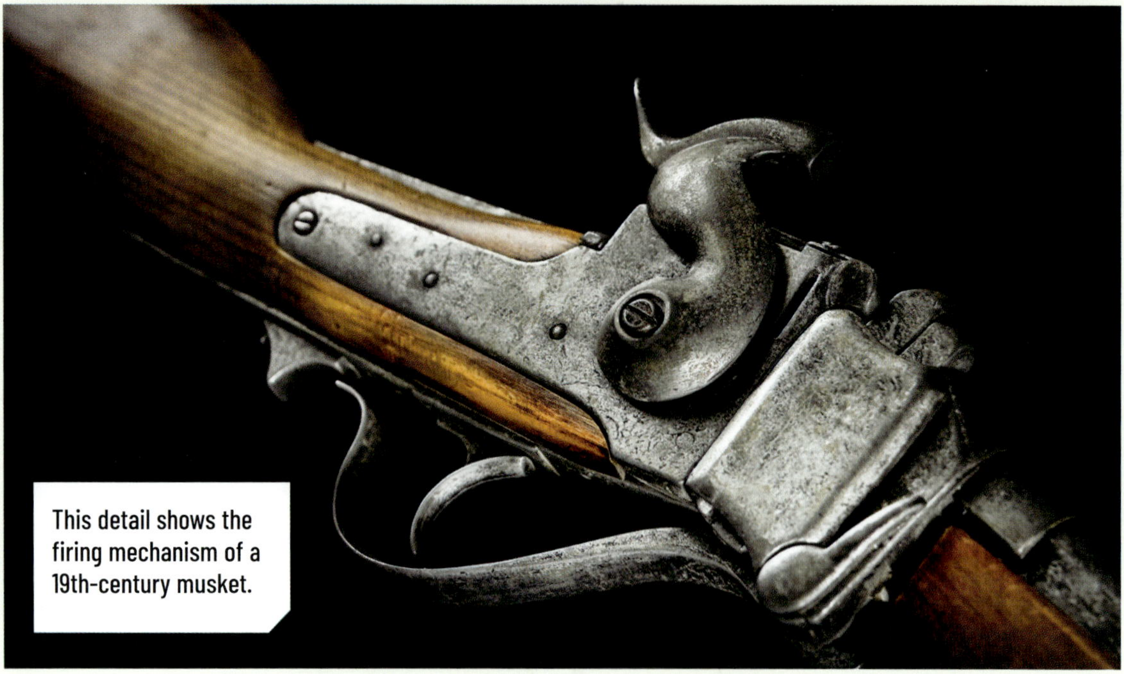

This detail shows the firing mechanism of a 19th-century musket.

TIMELINE
1430–1457

KEY:

Engineering and Technology

1430 The matchlock is introduced as the firing mechanism for small arms.

1442 German inventor Johannes Gutenberg sets up a printing press using movable type, the first in Europe.

1445 Portuguese shipbuilders develop the caravel; the ship is used by navigators over the next two centuries, including Christopher Columbus.

The origins of gunpowder are shrouded in mystery, mainly because the people who invented it wanted to keep it a secret. Gunpowder is a mixture of charcoal, sulfur, and saltpeter (potassium nitrate). When mixed in the correct proportions it burns rapidly, with 40 percent of the products being gases and the remainder solids in the form of smoke. The hot gases expand; if confined inside a container, they explode with a loud bang. If burned at the closed end of an open-ended tube, the expanding hot gases will push out a ball or bullet, which is the principle of the cannon and all firearms.

Early Steps with Gunpowder

With the advent of gunpowder, fireworks became popular in China in the 1100s. Fireworks often came in the form of strings of firecrackers; gunpowder bombs were more dangerous. Around 1220, the Chinese military made bombs with outer casings that shattered on explosion to kill or maim the enemy.

A Japanese woodcut of 1292 illustrates a bomb exploding, showing that gunpowder had reached

Timeline

c.1020 Invention of gunpowder

1044 First written mention of gunpowder

1100 Fireworks

1220 Gunpowder bombs

1242 Written description of gunpowder

1280 Gunpowder cannon

1375 Bronze cannon

1540 Cast-iron cannon

This pair of ornate flintlock pistols were made from brass and wood.

1450 European metalworkers learn to separate silver from lead ores such as galena.

1451 German cleric Nicholas of Cusa prescribes eyeglasses with concave lenses for nearsighted people.

1450 | 1451 | 1453 | 1457

1453 At the Siege of Constantinople (now Istanbul), Ottoman forces employ a huge cannon that fires cannonballs weighing up to 1,345 pounds (610 kg).

1457 The first passenger coach, with suspension, is built at Kocs in Hungary (and named after the town).

Berthold Schwarz

Berthold Schwarz was a famous semi-legendary character of the 14th century. He is often said to have been a monk and alchemist who lived in Germany in about 1320. He was nicknamed Schwarz ("black") because of the thick smoke that surrounded his primitive chemical experiments, and he is credited with the invention of gunpowder in Europe. The composition of the explosive was first described in writing in Europe by English scientist Roger Bacon (c.1214–1292) in 1242.

A war reenactor fires a matchlock musket by using a fuse to light the powder.

Japan by then. There is a reference to saltpeter and rockets in a 1280 book on warfare from Syria. The gunpowder cannon turns up in the late 1280s, when the Chinese military used them. Around 1300, Arab technicians made cannon barrels from bamboo tubes. Metal barrels made from a bundle of wrought-iron rods were bound with iron. In 1346, the English used wrought-iron cannons, called bombards, against the French, and a year later European gunsmiths made arrow-firing cannons. German gunsmiths cast the first cannon barrels as a single piece of bronze in 1378. Bronze was chosen, especially for ships' cannons, because it does not corrode as easily as iron. French gunners used cast iron to make cannonballs from about 1495, and cast-iron barrels were first made in England in the mid-16th century.

Personal Weapons

The first "small arm" was invented in Spain in the mid-1400s. The shooter propped the barrel on a support, firing the weapon from the shoulder. The gunpowder charge was put in the barrel and lit with a lighted match. The musket replaced this within 100 years and the

TIMELINE
1461–1496

KEY:

Life Sciences

Engineering and Technology

Astronomy and Math

1461 1464 1473

1461 Breech-loading cannons are first used in Europe.

1464 German mathematician Regiomontanus writes an overview of trigonometry.

1473 In Italy, the first European version of *The Cannon of Medicine* by the Persian physician Avicenna is published.

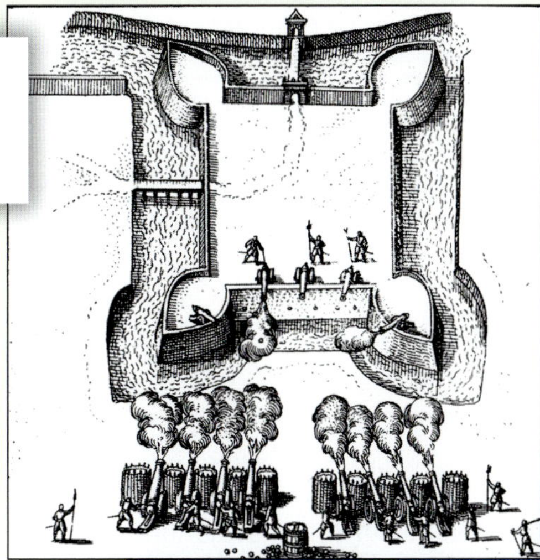

This illustration from the 17th century shows cannons being used to besiege a fortress. As cannons improved, so the design of defenses improved.

flintlock replaced the matchlock. To fire a flintlock, the musketeer poured gunpowder down the muzzle, followed by a lead ball. He rammed a felt wad in to keep the ball and charge in place. He then put some fine powder in the pan at the side of the lock, and pulled back the cock, which held a piece of flint. As he pulled the trigger, the flint hit the steel and made sparks that ignited the powder in the pan. This lit the main charge, and the musket went off.

The musket had a smooth bore; it gave way to the rifle, which had a spirally grooved barrel to give a spin to the ball or bullet. Further developments led to the breech-loading rifle and cartridges. Handguns followed the same pattern, going from muzzle-loading flintlock pistols to cartridge weapons. Another advance was the introduction of multishot revolvers.

From 1543, cannons were made from cast iron, reducing the risk of the barrels exploding.

1482 Italian mathematician Johannes Campanus translates Euclid's *Elements* into Latin.

1485 Italian artist and inventor Leonardo da Vinci produces a design for a parachute.

1492 Italian navigator Christopher Columbus sails across the Atlantic to islands in the Caribbean.

1494 Italian mathematician Luca Pacioli describes double-entry bookkeeping, the basis of all modern accounting.

1496 England's King Henry VII establishes the length of the standard yard and sets other weights and measures.

1482 1485 1492 1494 1496

Glossary

alchemy An early form of chemistry; alchemists tried to cure all diseases and to turn base metals into gold.

algebra The branch of mathematics that studies the properties of mathematical structures, and in which unknown quantities are denoted by letters.

astrolabe An early navigational device for measuring the height of the sun, from which the time could be calculated.

astronomy The study of objects outside Earth's atmosphere.

caliph A Muslim leader.

compass A navigational device with a pivoted magnetized needle that always swings to point to magnetic north.

escapement In clocks and watches, a mechanism that controls the regular release of energy from a falling weight or coiled spring.

flintlock A mechanism used to ignite the charge in a muzzle-loading pistol or musket; the trigger produces a spark from the flint, which ignites the charge.

gears Toothed cogs used to transmit rotary motion from one part of a machine to another.

geometry The branch of mathematics that studies the properties of shapes.

gunpowder An explosive mixture of powdered carbon (charcoal), saltpeter (potassium nitrate), and sulfur.

lodestone A piece of the mineral magnetite, which has magnetic properties (it attracts iron or steel).

magnetic north The direction indicated by the needle of a compass; it is not quite the same as true north.

matchlock A type of early firing mechanism for a musket, using an S-shaped piece of metal holding a fuse.

optics The science of light and vision.

portolan chart An early European navigational chart showing coastlines and place names.

Renaissance A cultural movement (the word means "rebirth") that began in Italy in the 14th century and spread through Europe by the 16th century.

trigonometry The branch of mathematics that deals with angles and triangles.

waterwheel An early device to harness the energy of flowing water.

Further Information

Books

Deadly History. The Vikings. Raids of Terror and Bloody Battles. Lerner Publishing Group, 2023.

Explore. Knights Through the Ages. Lerner Publishing Group, 2024.

Falk, Seb. *The Light Ages: The Surprising Story of Medieval Science.* W. W. Norton and Coy, 2020.

Graphic Science Biographies. Avicenna and the Book of Medicine. Lerner Publishing Group, 2023.

Wheeler, E. B. *Mysteries of the Middle Ages: True Stories from the Medieval World.* Rowan Ridge Press, 2023.

Woods, Michael and Mary B. Woods. *Machines Through the Ages. From Furnaces to Factories (Technology Through the Ages).* Lerner, 2024.

Woods, Michael and Mary B. Woods. *Agriculture Through the Ages. From Silk to Supermarkets (Technology Through the Ages).* Lerner Publishing Group, 2024.

Websites

www.historyforkids.net/middle-ages.html?utm_content=cmp-true
Web site introducing all aspects of life in the Middle Ages, with information on daily life, people and nations, and weapons and warfare.

www.thecollector.com/medieval-period-science-facts/
Five facts about science in the medieval period explained, with illustrations and links to other relevant information.

www.medievalchronicles.com/medieval-history/medieval-inventions-list/
Comprehensive list of important medieval inventions, with links to informative articles and illustrations.

pressbooks.pub/anne1/chapter/the-medieval-world-and-sts/
Science, Technology, and Society, a student-led exploration of science in the Middle Ages.

Publisher's note to educators and parents: Our editors have carefully reviewed these websites to ensure that they are suitable for students. Many websites change frequently, however, and we cannot guarantee that a site's future contents will continue to meet our high standards of quality and educational value. Be advised that students should be closely supervised whenever they access the internet.

Index